Hair Artist Lifestyle

Summer 2014 Edition

I0300678

The Secret Formula for
Creating Personal Goals that Improve Your Results

Add-On Treatments Boost Salon Revenue

Fun Haircolor Without The Chemicals

HOW TO Market on Instagram

Visit www.HAALifestyleMag.com

And More Inside...

CONTENTS

Summer 2014 Edition

A Letter from the Editor page 3

Beauty page 5

Add-On Treatments Boost Salon Revenue

Fun Haircolor Without The Chemicals

Great Results For Every Smile

Feed Your Hair

Create New Shades of Perfection

Business page 28

How to Market on Instagram

How to Incorporate YouTube into Your Beauty Salon Business

Lifestyle page 32

Living Pretty With Your Busy Lifestyle

The Secret Formula for Creating Personal Goals that Improve Your Results

Letter from Editor

I am very excited to present to you the Summer 2014 Edition of Hair Artist Lifestyle Magazine. I sincerely thank all of our contributors, editors and you for helping to make this possible.

Every year we celebrate another year of life. We make special plans for the day and appreciate knowing that on this one day in the year, our life becomes the focus of the significant people with who we are privileged to share our life. There is a child inside all of us when it comes to the celebration of our birthday, with its sense of fun, of friendship and of celebration of all that is good.

Someone once said that it is a shame that we can't have a birthday every day. How true are those words? We put so much time and energy into preparations for that day. Imagine if every day of our lives was spent with the same feeling of preparation and anticipation. Seize the Day is a saying made popular in movies, but it's equally applicable in our lives. When was the last time you lived each day as if it was potentially your last day on this earth and packed it full of experiences, celebrations, friendship and fun?

We often let days pass without really thinking too much about how we spend them. Weeks pass without us realizing how many wasted opportunities we have let slip past us because we are so focused on surviving the day and all we try to pack into it.

Try to re focus your life this week. Take a few minute at the beginning of the week to put a plan into action that reflects the things and the people that are important to you. Create some short-term goals of things you would like to see accomplished with week and plan a celebration with family and friends for a week from today.

As each day ends, look at the goals or the ideas you had for that day and ask yourself if you accomplished them. Reflect on how they affected you and what they added to your life and how good they made you feel. Allow your inner self to be reborn as you reflect with excitement the beautiful butterfly you saw when you went on your walk, or the delightful coffee you had with a work colleague you hadn't seen in a while.

As for the weekends, call your family and friends around you and celebrate together not just your birthday, but also your week of rebirth days, and make this a life habit.

Add-On Treatments Boost Salon Revenue!

You can add value to your client's salon services while dramatically boosting your service tickets and retail by offering add-on salon and spa service treatments. Add-on treatments will also help you work smarter, creating more balance in your life. Perhaps you can shorten your day or your week with the additional revenue you'll earn, or just plan a great vacation or a big splurge!

Revenue Boost: Prepare yourself for added income! Let's say you have a basic add-on treatment that costs $20 and you do just two a day. In a week's time, you will have made $200 above your baseline. Over a 50-week period you've totaled $10,000 above baseline—all without adding any additional clients! To really increase your profits from add-ons, start planning them into your day. Think about which clients would benefit from specific add-ons, then plan ahead to upsell. Let's say you have 150 regular clients and their average ticket is $65. If you bump it up only $10 more, then over a typical five week period until you see the clients again, you will have increased your income by $1,500. Over a 50 week period that easily becomes $15,000.

Add-On Choices: Consider which add-on treatments will blend well with your salon offerings. If you specialize in hair color, you could feature add-on glossing treatments, deep conditioning treatments, or scalp treatments for healthier hair. To add a bit of the spa to your salon, consider a full head massage with a hair mask or oil, pressure point facial massage, or an aromatherapy treatment. ESS® Aromatherapy from Universal Companies offers pure essential oil based formulations for all of your aromatherapy needs. You could even offer complimentary mini treatments to introduce a more complete add-on service. For example, to pique client interest in aromatherapy, you may want to offer a free aroma spritz at the beginning of each appointment and explain that you offer an optional add-on for a full aromatherapy experience.

Wax Hair Removal: Waxing is a very simple, fast, and profitable add-on service and is a staple for salons. Offer eyebrow and upper lip waxing for every client. If your salon also offers full spa waxing, this may stimulate the interest of clients to try a full service later. The Plum Smooth® Waxing System by Universal Companies contains extra virgin plum seed oil, an antioxidant oil that absorbs quickly to nourish, moisturize, and improve skin elasticity. Plum Smooth waxes melt at lower temperatures for faster services and come in larger 16 ounce cans, giving you more product for a lower cost. The Plumb Smooth waxing line also offers home care products for retailing, including Plumb Genius™ for ingrown hair and razor rash, Plumb Calm™ tea tree oil for inflamed skin, and Plumb Numb™ for pre-treatment comfort.

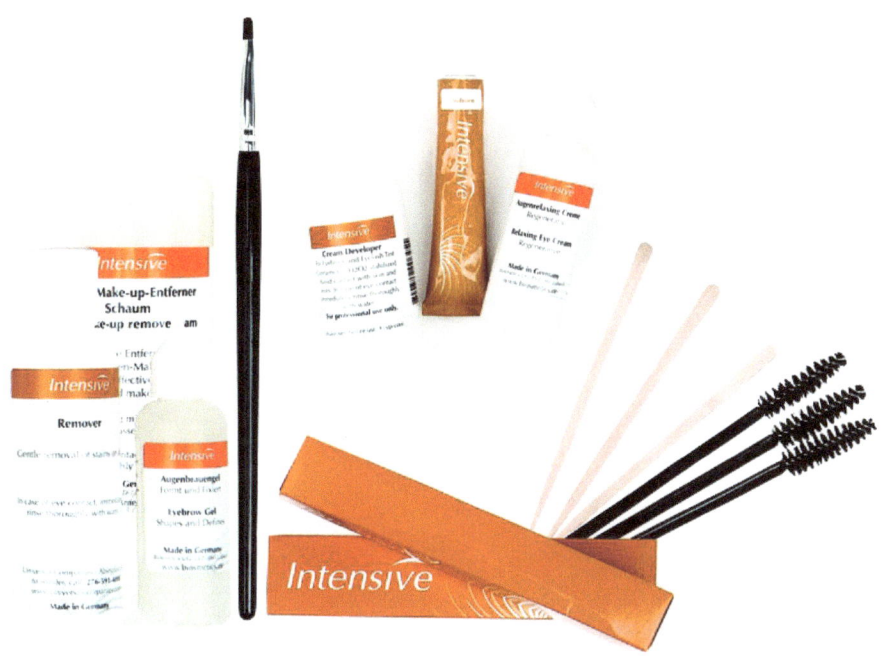

Lash Services: Lash and brow tinting is one of the most popular and profitable services you can offer in your business and it is the perfect add-on service. In just 15 minutes, you will give clients spectacular lashes with a safe, easy-to-use lash tinting service that offers effective and dramatic long-lasting results. Universal Companies offers Intensive Lash & Brow Tint®, which comes in eight basic tint colors. Mixing the colors offers a wide variety of shade options, creating endless possibilities and customized looks for your clients. A pre-packaged Success Kit® comes fully stocked with enough products for hundreds of treatments. This can generate up to $10,500, with the cost per treatment of only .53 cents. Creating a "Lash & Brow Bar" in your reception area will attract clients on their way in and out of your business and create curb appeal.

Eco-Friendly: For a taste of the spa, offer your clients hand and foot treatments that are also eco-friendly and cost saving for you! Universal Companies' Eco-fin® treatments are a natural, petroleum-free alternative to paraffin with a rich blend of palm, soy, jojoba, organic coconut oils, shea butter, vitamin E, and essential oils. Eco-fin treatments are single use, taking just seconds for a sanitary and mess–free clean up. They are 100% disposable and biodegradable, keeping paraffin waste out of landfills. Conveniently packed in pre-measured cubes that come in an array of delectable fragrances, each tray contains 40 cubes, enough for 20 sets of hand or foot treatments. A pre-packaged Eco-fin Success Kit comes fully stocked with enough products for 100+ treatments for hands or feet. This can generate up to $2,800 with the cost per treatment of only $2.49.

Boost Relaxation: If you are offering hair extension or hair braiding services to your clientele, they may be seated for two or more hours. As long as you have them in your chair for that long, why not offer additional services that enhance their relaxation? You can cross market with spa professionals in your salon to offer reflexology treatments, spa foot treatments, or massage. Additionally you could offer anti-aging hand treatments, manicures, and pedicure services. For a deep relaxation experience, offer energy work, guided visualization, sound therapy, or meditation.

With over 30 years of proven success, Universal Companies has become the leading single-source supplier to over 30,000 spa professionals in 47 countries. For more information on where to purchase Universal Companies products, call 800-558-5571 or visit www.UniversalCompanies.com.

Jenny Hogan is the Media Director at Marketing Solutions, Inc., a full-service marketing, advertising and PR agency specializing in the professional beauty and spa businesses. For more information, contact 407-395-9007, visit www.MktgSols.com or send an email to MktgSols@MktgSols.com.

Fun Haircolor Without The Chemicals

Create Spectacular Salon Haircolor Without Damaging Your Client's Hair Or The Environment

The quickest way to achieve haircolor without damaging your client's hair and the environment is with professional hair extensions. Di Biase Hair Extensions USA offers hair extensions that are safe for your client's health without causing repercussions to the ecosystem.

Vikki Parman, CEO for Di Biase Hair Extensions USA shares, "Hair extensions are the perfect way to help introduce highlights or fantasy colors to your clients, without any bleach or haircolor chemistry. The fantasy haircolor options are a great addition for a fun look during any party or special event. Try one streak or multiple streaks for a fun new look that requires no bleach or harsh chemicals, meaning no damage to the client's hair. Many teens, athletes and fans of all ages like to have a few streaks of fantasy haircolor to go with their team colors for sporting events, class reunions, to match prom dresses as well as just for fun."

411 On Hair Color Dyes: Most clients have no idea what ingredients are in their hair dye, what those chemicals can do to their health and the environment. Clients look at the box and see a bunch of unpronounceable words. Worse yet, they may ask their hairstylist who only noncommittally shrugs. But why do clients chose to ignore products that could damage their health or the future of the ecosystem?

By taking a closer look at common ingredients in hair dyes, clients will gain a deeper understanding of why hair extensions are the safer choice when it comes to haircolor. One common component of hair dye is ammonia, which is an environmental toxin and highly harmful to aquatic life. The next chemicals that are quite common in dye are benzene, which is extremely toxic to the environment and coal tar.

Coal tar is a known carcinogen, highly toxic to the environment and has been banned in several states when used as a pavement sealcoat. Additionally, hair dyes contain lead acetate, which is bad for the environment and can result in lead poisoning. A common compound known as p-Phenylenediamine (PPD) and also referred to as p-Diaminobenzene, oxidation dye, amino dye and para dye, has strong links to cancer and is harmful to the environment, particularly marine life. Used to improve color adhesion and add gloss, is the environmentally toxic, toluene, which can increase cell mutations and cause cancer in animals. Repeated exposure can cause damage to the central nervous system, liver and kidneys.

Fun & Stylish Haircolor: Creative haircolor is a huge aspect of the most current hairstyle trends and will accent any great haircut. You will always be able to make a big difference in your clients' hair and image with haircolor artistry. An exciting new trend this year is haircolor without the use of chemicals. Semi-permanent and temporary hair extensions are among your clients' top choices for haircolor without chemicals. Fantasy haircolor shades have become a bigger trend in the past couple of years for fashionable women of all ages. Try some of the bold reds and blues to give your clients' hair an edgy appearance or for a softer look, there is an array of pastel options. There are always the more saturated bright haircolor shades that may be added in your salon with bonded, adhesive or clip-in hair extensions!

Parman notes, "When selling fantasy color hair extensions as a salon service and as a retail product, it is important for you and your entire staff to wear them. Try something different every few months to stay fashionable, while also creating something new to talk about during your client consultations. Whether you promote pink hair for Valentine's Day and for special October breast cancer events, the seasonal opportunities are endless. The client will observe the professional hair designer wearing them and then will realize the hair extensions must be safe for her hair as well. Wearing colorful hair extensions as accents will show off your fashionable options, as well as to build confidence in the professional new services that are being offered in your salon!"

Join The Extended Revolution! Di Biase Hair Extensions USA offers a wide variety of 100% human Remy hair extensions with bonded, adhesive and clip-in application techniques. For more information on Di Biase Hair Extensions USA as well as their certification workshops, introductory kits and products, call 248-885-4748 or email: Info@DiBiaseHairUSA.com. Visit: www.DiBiaseHairUSA.com.

Great Results For Every Smile!
Teeth Whitening Services Are The Perfect Add-on For Your Salon Clientele

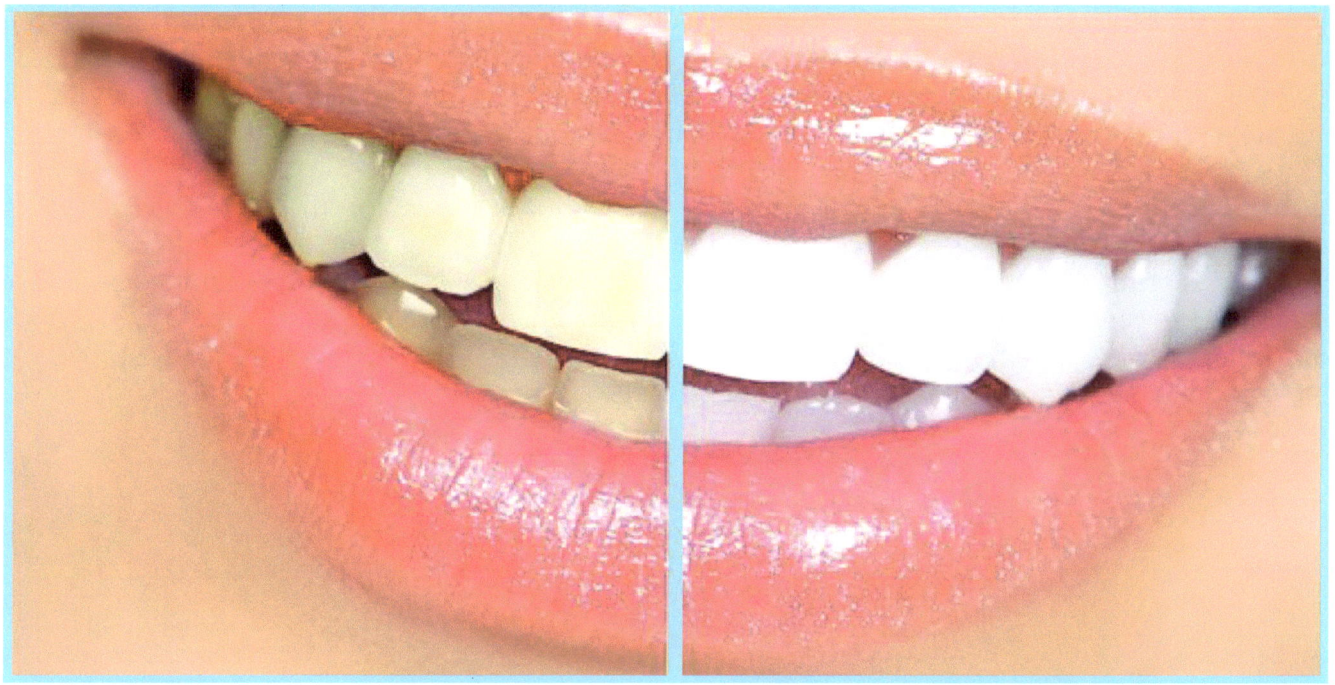

Teeth whitening continues to be a very popular and lucrative new salon and spa service, with the consumer whitening industry now worth $11 billion. Salons and spas can now offer clients this effective new professional service as an add-on or stand alone service for added value and increased revenue. Ronnie Weir, President of Laser Wellness PMA offers Whiter Brighter Smiles teeth whitening equipment and take-home kits for retailing. Weir says, "Our mission is to help improve the self-image of people, one smile at a time by providing effective teeth whitening treatments at an affordable price. Teeth whitening is the perfect addition to any salon or spa menu and will enhance your current services with fast and effective results."

Weir is now offering from 35 to 50% discounts for salons and spas who wish to invest in these lucrative new teeth whitening opportunities. Your salon can offer in-house services or retail take home kits with very little initial investment.

Enhanced Self Image: An attractive smile is a vital part of a healthy self-image and will instantly boost confidence, leaving a lasting impression. Studies show that 84% of adults perceive having an attractive smile as being important. A great smile enhances the ability to get a job, receive a promotion and to find love! When meeting new people, 85% consider a person's smile to be very or somewhat important and is one of the first qualities noticed. Almost 9 out 10 Americans report that people with good teeth are more attractive. A vital part of a good smile is having whiter, brighter teeth and the confidence to flash a wide grin!

Easy Esthetic Makeovers: Today, teeth whitening can be performed simply and quickly in any spa setting. A whitening agent consisting of hydrogen peroxide gel is applied to the teeth. Then an LED lamp emitting cold blue light is placed directly in front of the teeth to accelerate the whitening process. The whitening process takes from 15 to 20 minutes with visible results in just one treatment, depending upon the severity of staining. Clients should receive at least 2 to 3 sessions of teeth whitening with additional sessions to get the best and longest lasting results.

Gum Sensitivity: To avoid teeth or gum sensitivity, look for teeth whitening services using carbamide peroxide. Weir says, "Look for services using whitening gels that contain carbamide peroxide instead of hydrogen peroxide. Hydrogen peroxide breaks down faster and causes more sensitivity to teeth and gums. As the carbamide breaks down, it creates oxidation on the surface of the teeth, which then results in the teeth becoming whiter. Oxidation works to lift stains, yet does not make teeth more porous or cause sensitivity."

Perfect Add-on Services: Teeth whitening is the perfect add-on service as it is so easy and fast to perform. You can suggest a whitening treatment at the beginning or end of any salon or spa service. Have front desk personnel suggest teeth whitening while clients are checking in, or have them pre-book during their check out for their next visit. Instead of taking up valuable treatment room space, create a nook somewhere private in your spa. You could use a corner in your lounge area or even in your front reception or retail area to create curb appeal. Include a comfortable chair, relaxing music or a soothing meditation chant.

Client Contraindications: Most clients are good candidates for whitening services. As with all spa services, first ensure there are no medical contraindications. Clients should be sixteen or older, as whitening could irritate nerve endings on immature teeth. Clients should not be pregnant or nursing. Some clients may be allergic to peroxide or have sensitive teeth or gums. Clients should have good general dental heath with no periodontal disease. Teeth whitening will not work on dental restorations, crowns and veneers. Some clients' teeth may also be too stained for whitening or have discoloration due to medications. Be sure to check into your state and local laws to see if you are able to offer teeth whitening services in your salon or spa business.

Create Series Packages: Salon clients will have varying whitening results, so manage expectations by not over promising and by relaying that the best results will come from a series of treatments. Weir shares that his South Dakota walk-in clinic offers a single whitening session of 20 minutes for $150. A package of three whitening treatments are priced at $300, offering a savings of $150. Additionally, Weir offers a home whitening kit for $299 that includes a LED unit, mouthpiece and 3cc syringe of whitening agent. A daily maintenance whitening pen is also available for $29.95. Weir often offers a deep discount for clients booking a series, such as 50% off the second service booked.

Your salon can now significantly increase service tickets and retail revenue by offering teeth whitening services and home care kits. Weir says, "Teeth whitening is a great new service for your spa menu and can really boost your R.O.I. income. It can add significant profits from service and retail sales, build client referrals and give your clients a wonderful new look. Your smile is important and it can really improve your health and wellness to have a whiter, brighter smile!"

By partnering with Laser Wellness PMA, full-service salon, spa and wellness professionals are now able to provide special new signature service treatments as well as an exciting new retail sales program for at-home treatment protocols with a variety of laser devices. For more information on Whiter Brighter Smiles call 605-791-5230 or email WhiterBrighterSmiles@GMail.com.

Whiter Brighter Smiles is headquartered at 3625 5th Street ~ Suite 202, Rapid City, SD 57701 USA. All QLaser products are made here in the USA. Jenny Hogan is the Media Director at Marketing Solutions, Inc., a full-service marketing, advertising and PR agency specializing in the professional beauty business. For more information, contact 407-395-9007, visit www.MktgSols.com or send an email to MktgSols@MktgSols.com

Feed Your Hair!
Shaoé Haircare Secret Seven System Delivers Decadence With Lustrous Hair

Caviar may not be something you indulge in on a regular basis, yet you should definitely be indulging in it for your clients' haircare! The new Shaoé Haircare Secret Seven Complex pampers the hair with the world's best natural ingredients inspired by all seven corners of the world. Clients will be elevated with the privileged feel of this luxury haircare line that will make their hair look celebrity stunning. You will be offering a truly unique product line that will increase your revenue with a retailing boost and provide great results. Give your clients solutions that will awaken their hum-drum routine and feed their hair like they were at a banquet!

Secret Seven Infusion: There are seven wonders of the ancient world, seven days in a week, seven colors in the rainbow, seven musical notes in a scale and seven continents in the world. Inspired by the diversity and bounty of the world's best ingredients and by the mystical number seven, Shaoé Haircare formulated a unique new system based on healthy elements from across the globe that provide unparalleled haircare results. Josef and Shaun Settle developed the Shaoé Haircare complex after extensive travel and research.

Josef Settle relays, "Professional product lines that are developed around a single ingredient only address one aspect of the hair. Our approach is to repair and nourish the hair from the scalp to the ends for total treatment. We created a cocktail of special ingredients inspired from all seven continents, while searching for the finest plant-based ingredients on the planet!" The results are a haircare line that works synergistically as a total system to stimulate the scalp, smooth the hair cuticle, repair environmental damage, moisturize and purify the hair while adding intense shine and a radiant finish. As all of the products in the Shaoé Haircare System repair the hair with every use, each time the hair is styled it is also rejuvenated. Here is a run-down of their exclusive ingredient list:

French Caviar Oil: The French are renowned for their caviar used in luxury skincare lines. Now, this decadent oil infuses each Secret Seven complex product. Packed with amino acids, omega 3 essential fatty acids and vitamins, this powerful oil moisturizes brittle tresses, increases luster and sheen.

African Baobab Oil: The Baobab tree itself is known to retain as much as 30,000 gallons of water and live thousands of years, producing the rare fruit only every 25 years. This essential oil is not often found in haircare products due to cost; they have brought you the finest grade available of this special oil. It delivers intensive conditioning and moisture-retaining benefits to soothe dry scalps, smooth and moisturize.

South American Aloe Vera: For many years, people have used Aloe for its healing and mending properties and the best in the world comes from South America. Loaded with essential vitamins and minerals, Aloe can help maintain the hair's pH balance and restore strength, sheen, luster, and beauty. Soothes psoriasis, dandruff, helps promote hair growth and a healthy scalp.

Galanga Root: Drawn on the inspiration of Antarctica's harsh conditions of extreme sun, wind and cold, this Asian root shields the hair from environmental stress. Acting as a natural sun protectant and helping to prevent haircolor from fading, this superior ingredient will shield your tresses from everyday pollutants.

Swiss Dark Chocolate: Naturally, they turned instantly to the Swiss to give you this delightfully delicious and beneficial ingredient. There is no argument that Europe produces the finest chocolate on the planet. Besides a delicious aroma, they have mastered the formulation and delivery so the natural antioxidants and vitamins are able to deeply condition and rejuvenate scalp and hair.

Australian Eucalyptus Oil: Used in folklore medicine for thousands of years to nourish the scalp, eucalyptus oil stimulates circulation by providing blood flow to the root bulb, and is believed to make hair stronger with more elasticity and sheen.

Himalayan Goji Berries: The aroma of this berry is also known as the "Happy Berry" and helps to create a sense of well-being and optimism! Most commonly referred to as the "Super Fruit," this berry is loaded with trace minerals, amino acids and is a natural antioxidant that provides enormous benefits to the hair and scalp.

Healthy Haircare: The development of the professional haircare line resulted from personal need. After Shaun Settle fell ill to severe respiratory problems developed from the salon environment; she thought she may need to leave her professional haircare career. Instead, Shaun and husband Joseph Settle carefully researched all safe haircare ingredients and developed the new Secret Seven Complex product line. Shaun stopped having respiratory problems and staff and clients love the healthy new products inspired by the seven corners of the world! The new line includes products to address every client's needs for a variety of hair types and conditions.

Complete Product System: Products within the Secret Seven Collection include Opulent Curl Shine Cream, Sophisticated Smoothing Serum, Pristine and Purifying Hair Cleanse, Decadent & Restorative Leave-in Conditioner, Avant Garde Thickening Paste, Rejuvenating Bliss Styling Cream, Radiant Texturizing Hair Polish and Crème de la Crème Setting Spray. Shaoé Haircare fuses the decadence of a privileged lifestyle with the provocative nature of fashion. Josef and Shaun Settle are known as nationally respected salon industry platform artists as well as the successful owners of Avant Gard the Salon & Spa and Avant Gard The School in Indianapolis, Indiana. With over 25 years of experience, they are sharply focused on the creation of dynamic hair artistry while also helping train as many other hair designers as possible.

Celebrate V.I.P Style With Shaoé Haircare! The new Shaoé Haircare system offers luxurious opulence for your client's hair. For more information on educational opportunities as well as to order Shaoé Haircare System products, call 317-272-1149, 855-YShaoé7 / 855-974-2637 or email: Info@ShaoeHaircare.com. Visit: www.ShaoeHaircare.com.

Create New Shades Of Perfection!
Chromastics Hair Color Presents No Lift, No Ammonia, No MEA ~ Liquid Hair Color

New Chromastics Shades has recently been launched as the next and newest step in the evolution of professional hair color. Shades is a deposit-only hair color system that has been perfectly designed for the most beautiful toning, glazing, refreshing and corrective hair color services. With the addition of Chromastics XL-Cream to your formula, Shades can be transformed into a beautiful base-breaker.

Tom Dispenza, president of Chromastics notes, "Chromastics Liquid Shades was created for much longer lasting color than was currently available for toning highlights and double process blonding. With Shades; you will discover excellent hair color blends with perfect coverage.

As with all professional Chromastics Hair Color products; Shades contain hydrolyzed wheat and rice protein to leave the hair looking and feeling great. Shades has a lower pH and works with just 10-volume developer. It processes up to 35 minutes. To make it even more versatile, when mixed with Chromastics XL-S and 20-volume developer, it becomes a base-breaker, eliminating the need to carry a special product to "break the base". It is more gentle than regular hair color. As a deposit only hair color, it will only add pigment to the hair. It is not meant to lighten the hair. You can also re-color hair often with minimal damage. With fifteen intermixable Shades plus clear, it is ideal for any salon."

Toning, Glazing, Refreshing & Corrective Haircolor: You will be able to mix equal parts of Chromastics Shades into an applicator bottle with 10 volume developer. Apply to shampooed and towel dried hair. Process for 5 to 30 minutes. Voila!

Creativity With Shades' Base-Breakers: To transform Chromastics Shades to a soft half level base-breaker, you will need to mix 2 ounces of Chromastics Shades and 2 ounces of 10-volume developer into an applicator bottle. Just add one-half ounce of XL-Cream. Then, rapidly apply this formula to new hair growth. Process for 10 to 15 minutes. To achieve a full level of lifting action, merely replace Chromastics XL-Cream with a half-ounce of XL-Super to achieve a full level of lift. Clear may also be used to lighten and dilute any shade. Chromastics Concentrates may also be added to further customize any formula. Heat is not recommended with Chromastics Shades.

Chromastics Shades For Relaxed and Straightened Hair: When coloring hair that has been relaxed or straightened, you must always be concerned with the fragility of the hair. African-American hair usually resembles a twisted oval rod. The hair fibers tend to twist along the length and often form narrow segments. These narrow segments then become the weakest part of the hair, especially after relaxing the hair. The melanin of the hair has been sensitized by the relaxing product and reacts faster to coloring or lightening chemicals. Chromastics Liquid Shades is ideal for relaxed or straightened hair. It has a much lower pH, 8.0, than permanent color and is mixed with 10-volume developer. Chromastics Liquid Shades Light Neutral Brown and Light Golden Brown are also perfect for blending or covering relaxed "gray" hair. The 4 hydrolyzed proteins of Chromastics Liquid Shades inclusive of silk, keratin, rice and wheat, make it ideal for building strength into the relaxed hair. All of the 15 Liquid Shades can be intermixed to create custom hair color for relaxed hair.

No MEA & Ammonia: Chromastics Hair Color is creatively designed with organic chemistry. Organic chemistry is based on combinations of carbon, hydrogen, oxygen and nitrogen. Chromastics uses no carcinogens that will damage your hair. Shades was designed without using MEA / ethanolamine. It has been infused with superior hydrolyzed proteins that include silk, keratin, rice and wheat. Each provides a unique strengthening characteristic. With Chromastics Shades, you will still safely achieve predictable hair color longevity, vibrancy and gray coverage without MEA or ammonia.

Chromastics Is The Future Evolution Of Hair Color: Peter Ciotti, CEO of Chromastics notes, "We continue to successfully grow by educating our professional hair colorists with superior information. We teach our affiliated hair colorists how to achieve the very best results with a smaller inventory investment and while using fewer products. Hair colorists have the advantage of knowing that with Chromastics, they will be able to replicate any color they or their client sees and wants. We also know that no one can duplicate your creative work, because you will always be able to create the customized hair color formulas for each client. Our Chromastics hair colorists are trained on how to create personalized designs that will always be the perfect hair color formulation for each client."

Shades Of Perfection! Chromastics President Tom Dispenza adds, "Chromastics puts complete artistic control back into the hands of the professional hair colorist. We understand and respect that the hair colorist needs to creatively control the deposit, the lightening and the tone of every hair color formula which should be customized for each salon client. Every shade of Chromastics Hair Color contains hydrolyzed proteins that will dramatically help the hair feel and look better."

Create Your Own Haircolor Evolution~ With Shades Of Excellence! For more information on Chromastics Shades Hair Color or to register for a regional hair color education workshop, call 818-735-7375 or 877-716-2889, email Tom@Chromastics.com. The Chromastics Hotline is always available at 917-375-7741. Visit www.Chromastics.com to sign up for their free newsletter. Larry Oskin is the Media Director at Marketing Solutions, Inc., a full-service marketing, advertising and PR agency specializing in the professional beauty business. For more information, contact 703-359-6000, visit www.MktgSols.com or send an email to LOskin@MktgSols.com

How to Market on Instagram

As Instagram becomes more and more popular, it is natural that smart businesses will devise ways to use it for their purposes. While we're not sure how long this will last, as Instagram is now owned by Facebook and change is inevitable, for the moment it is killing it's social parent when it comes to engagement.

Witness the recent (2014) study by Forrester Research that shows among other things, that Instagram is whipping its parent Facebook in terms of user engagement by a measly 60X! Add Facebook's recent trimming of marketer's sails in regards to organic ad reach, and you can see why everyone is actively looking to see what Instagram is capable of doing for their brand. Here are 7 ways we've found that http://blog.wishpond.com/post/59612395517/52-tips-how-to-market-on-instagram companies are using Instagram to help with their social marketing.

7 Ways to market your Beauty Salon Business on Instagram

Get a business account on Instagram - Making sure you have a branded business account is the very first step, along with completing your company profile and connecting it to Facebook and other social media channels.

Don't be shy about using hashtags - Use hashtags in your updates, as that is a major part of how people find you using mobile. Likewise, use your brand hashtags and make sure to monitor these, as you'll want to catch any comments or concerns before they explode.

Engage your customers - Like your followers photos, comment, embed, mention and otherwise recognize and engage with those connected to you.

Employ Instagram's new video function - Create some innovative 15-second videos to showcase your products and brand.

Show off your products - Instagram is a fantastic way to get your products some wide reaching audience they may not have had.

Use Crowdsourcing to create excitement about your products - Set up a contest and ask users to submit their best images of your products, showing their best uses and results.

Post frequently - Find your optimum posting rate, whether that is a few times a week or more than once a day. The key is to post enough that your audience is growing and engaging. You'll know it when you see it.

Charlotte Howard is a Woman Entrepreneur, 5x's Best Selling Author, CEO of Charlotte Howard Consulting, LLC, CEO & Founder of Hair Artist Association, LLC, CEO of Heart Centered Women Publishing, Publisher of Hair Artist Lifestyle Magazine and Founding Premier Member of Women Speakers Association. Charlotte is an Internationally renown Radio Host for Success & Beauty Talk Radio Show.

Charlotte is also a certified Award-winning Hair Artist with over a decade of experience specializing in Women Transformational Life Coaching, Beauty Care Strategies, Hair Artistry, Beauty Salon Business Start-up, Marketing and Client Attraction. She is on a mission to empower millions of women to discover fulfillment and happiness in their lives. She is all about women empowering women to create a renewed sense of energy and motivation for enhancing themselves, lives and business from the inside out! For more information visit www.thehairartistassociation.org

How to Incorporate YouTube into Your Beauty Salon Business

YouTube is now the second largest search engine on the planet, and by far the most flexible. You can embed YouTube videos quickly and easily just about anywhere, and multiply your marketing efforts with ease. Additionally, using YouTube marketing in your business is an extremely cost-effective way to drive traffic and sales. You've heard the stats touting YouTube as the behemoth it is, and the reasons you really need to use it in your business. Nevertheless, it's not always clear exactly how to go about that.

Let's look at 7 ways you can incorporate YouTube into your business quickly and profitably.

1. **Create videos of your products and services** - Here's your chance to demonstrate your stuff in action. Strive to make these videos fun, and not overly technical. Emphasize what benefits they can give to the buyers.

2. **Drive lots of traffic** - Videos can drive LOTS of traffic! Make sure you properly optimize your YouTube videos, and learn the specifics of what it takes to rank them well. Just so you know, it's far easier to rank a video compared to a web page. Something to think about.

3. **Create a dedicated YouTube channel for your brand** - Making a specific YouTube channel for your business will help in many ways, particularly in Google rankings. YouTube is also a social network, so you would be wise to keep watch over any comments that pop up on your videos and channel.

4. **Put a face on your business** - Letting people meet you and some of your staff by way of video is a marvelous way to build trust.

5. **Create short videos of valuable tips** - Create tip videos that demonstrate your expertise in various areas your audience has an interest in.

6. **Link to your videos with social media** - These days it's very important to link our properties together, so that you can create not only better search rankings, but also social media traffic. Make sure you include links on your social media sites!

7. **Use clients and customer testimonials** - A fantastic way to showcase both your clients and customers, (who'll become raving fans!) and provide social proof regarding your products and services.

Charlotte Howard is a Woman Entrepreneur, 5x's Best Selling Author, CEO of Charlotte Howard Consulting, LLC, CEO & Founder of Hair Artist Association,LLC, CEO of Heart Centered Women Publishing, Publisher of Hair Artist Lifestyle Magazine and Founding Premier Member of Women Speakers Association. Charlotte is an Internationally renown Radio Host for Success & Beauty Talk Radio Show.

Charlotte is also a certified Award-winning Hair Artist with over a decade of experience specializing in Women Transformational Life Coaching, Beauty Care Strategies, Hair Artistry, Beauty Salon Business Start-up, Marketing and Client Attraction. She is on a mission to empower millions of women to discover fulfillment and happiness in their lives. She is all about women empowering women to create a renewed sense of energy and motivation for enhancing themselves, lives and business from the inside out! For more information visit www.thehairartistassociation.org

Living Pretty With Your Busy Lifestyle
Tips & Tricks To Help Maintain Your Hair, Nails & Skin After Salon Visits

With the rise of technology, clients are always on the go for work and play. They are seeking new solutions to keep their appearance looking fresh and fabulous. With over 30 years of experience, Maggie Lopez Sales, Senior Hairstylist at David's Beautiful People in North Bethesda, Maryland, offers hair tips to clients whose schedules are demanding. Professional makeup artist Faye Mendelsohn also addresses how to keep skin looking youthful and how to apply makeup in 5 minutes.

Tips To Maintain Clients' Hair After A Salon Visit: Prior to gently shampooing their hair and following up with a warm water, rinse and add a neutralizing conditioner. Keeping your client's hair in good condition is paramount. Excessive cleaning may rob the hair of moisture and elasticity. Suggest to clients that they use a quality conditioner on porous areas. Inform clients to remove most of the moisture from the hair with a towel before blowing dry with a round brush. Make sure the client is using a hairbrush that is either a natural bristle or has bristles with a coated round-tip.

Blow dry using natural boar bristle brushes. Having the hair clarified and conditioned as preparation for the haircolor service will provide balanced coverage that lasts. I highly recommend using the Chromastics Clarifying Shampoo and Conditioner Extreme while applying the color on damp hair. To add volume and waves without the use of hot tools, it is ideal to use Velcro rollers immediately following the blow dry, while the hair cools. Clients seeking to create long lasting, bouncier curls should let the hair dry naturally or overnight after applying a styling product. The hair can then be curled using electric sticks or rollers and allowed to cool. A curling iron or flat iron can also be used to form waves, curls or ringlets. If a client wants more body and a hard hold, they should back brush the roots and smooth the surface to achieve maximum height and hold after they remove the rollers. At David's Beautiful People, we offer a solution to dry hair with the Nano Keratin Treatment, which will help client's with hydration issues and recommend our signature D-Line to help keep their hair follicles well hydrated.

Suggestions To Keep Haircolor Looking Vibrant: I recommend the client wait a few days prior to gently shampooing their hair and limit the cleansing and rinsing thereafter. Shampooing once with water on a low temperature and using a haircolor safe product is advisable. As for haircolor options, consider Chromastics Hair Color, an organic hair color with ingredients that are combined to create every shade. Encourage your clients to avoid "color zappers" after their haircolor treatment. Water is a huge problem and considered a color zapper as water removes a lot of haircolor from the hair shaft. Avoid harsh shampoos, UV rays, chlorine, mineral water and products containing alcohol and sulfate. Keep the use of hot hairstyling tools to a minimum. Remind clients that perms and relaxers may also remove haircolor. They should use haircolor safe moisturizers and follow with a cold rinse.

Preventative Measures & Care For Nails: Remind your clients to keep their nails dry, as water can be very damaging to the nail bed and cuticle. If it is impossible for clients to keep their hands out of water, remind them to dry their hands as often as possible. Make sure clients are using an acetone free nail polish remover. It is highly suggested that clients do not pick or bite their nails, because the bacteria will affect the nail bed and it will yield brittle nails. I suggest moisturizing their nails and cuticles with lanolin lotion and keeping the corners of the nails rounded. Gel manicures last a couple of weeks. They do no chip or peel and the client will have a nice manicure that lasts.

Youthful Looking Skin: In recent years BB Cream, a lightweight sheen type of cream with broad spectrum SPF 30, has become very popular on the market. It is wonderful for all skin types because it gives a beautiful youthful finish without feeling like greasy in any way. People love that cream because it is sheer, so it is good for all ages. It can be used with a type of heavier foundation for clients who need more coverage. It can also be used on teenagers who don't want coverage, but want the skin protection and a pretty look. I call it a "pretty sunscreen", because it is exactly that. It gives their skin an iridescence and radiance. This is the most popular product at Faye Mendelsohn Cosmetics. I highly suggest their BB cream for clients seeking a youthful look.

Makeup In 5 Minutes: First, consider the canvas. The canvas is the base on which the color is applied. The canvas includes concealer, foundation, a moisture tint, a BB Crème or for more coverage a foundation and a lightweight powder. The goal is to conceal before you enhance. By far the most important thing is at least two minutes should be designated for preparation of the canvas. There are color selections that are neutral, which go on all skin tones. I have those listed on www.FayeCosmetics.com for clients to select colors that are good for their particular skin tones. I advise them personally on placement of color. The same color of blush used for casual makeup can also be used for dressy occasions. I usually keep them within 1 to 2 shades of the neutral color, such as beige. For eyeliner, use a gel liner, which is long lasting and only requires a few touch ups during the day. This can be the same for lipstick. Use products that are long lasting and that only require a little gloss during the day to refresh the color. It should not take much more than 5 minutes to look absolutely great!

David's Beautiful People: David's Beautiful People is recognized as an industry leader by Intercoiffure, a respected international organization of top salons for achievements in the industry. Founded by David Cohen, David's Beautiful People was named "Top Salon" by *Washingtonian Magazine* and other local publications over the past 14 years as well as "Top Hair Colour Salon" by Celebrity *101 Hairstyles Magazine* and one of the 'Top 200 Salons In America' by *American Salon* magazine for its dynamic group of hairstylists and haircolourists. Additional *Washingtonian Magazine* accolades include 'Best Salon', 'Best Evening Hairstyles', 'Best Haircolor Salon', 'Best Hair Extensions Salon' and 'Best Thermal Relaxers'. David's Beautiful People has been a consistent 'Best of Bethesda Award' winner over the past few years.

For more information about David's Beautiful People, contact 301-881-2540 or visit www.DavidsBeautifulPeople.com. Visit them at:12121 Rockville Pike, North Bethesda, MD 20852 USA. Larry Oskin is the Media Director at Marketing Solutions, Inc., a full-service marketing, advertising and PR agency specializing in the professional beauty business. For more information, contact 703-359-6000, visit www.MktgSols.com or send an email to LOskin@MktgSols.com

The Secret Formula for Creating Personal Goals that Improve Your Results

In life, we have a formula to use that helps us to create goals that assist us in improving our personal life. To start these goals however, we must use our inner qualities. The inner qualities include skills, ability to commit, ability to set priorities, ability to accept failure, will to say no, and so on. We have self-awareness, personality and other details within as well that helps us to find ways to improve our personal life.

Once you find your qualities, develop them you will find it easy to set goals. To get started consider brainstorming, long-term goals, short-term goals, evaluation of these goals, brainstorming some more, evaluating, and so on. You want to consider managing your time as well.

When you brainstorm you, develop new ideas. New ideas is the market that leads you to success. Brainstorming helps you to learn something new. When you start to brainstorm you, begin seeing things you didn't see before. When you brainstorm, it is wise to take notes. The notes will help you to remember things you had forgotten. Use the notes to structure your plans.

As you sit and write be sure to start your plans with short-term goals. The short-term goals should lead up to your long-term goals. Short-term goals should include what you want to accomplish in the next few years. Do you plan to open a business? Do you plan to move? Do you plan to start a new career. Each question will lead you into the right direction as you find answers.

For instance, I plan to open a business in the next few years. How do you plan to open that business? What business are you considering? How will you get the money to start your business. You have many options, so check your resources, learn new resources and continue building your dreams to improve your personal life.

After you layout the plans for your short-term dreams, start working toward your long-term goals. For instance, in the next ten years what do you see yourself doing? Use your visions and voices inside to cultivate a plan. Brainstorm your ideas.

To set up long-term plans keep them realistic. Make sure that your long-term falls in accord with your short-term goals. For instance, if you plan to start a business in the next few years, build on this dream and plan to become productive and established in the near future. Start saving money to back your plans. You will need to set up a budget that allows you money to save.

How to budget:

Your budget is based on your net income. If make $30,000 per year, set a budget that works within your means. Set aside money for backup, recovery, and money to save. Perhaps you can also include in your plans a trip to the Internet. On the Internet and at your local library or colleges you will find that many grants are available to those starting a new business.

How to save time:

You will need a time plan. You will need to plan your time wisely. The more time you plan to save the faster you will reach your dreams to improve your personal life and reach your goals. Save time by reviewing your daily activities, entertainment, family time, work time, leisure time and so on. If you spend four hours watching television, reduce your time to save by viewing television one hour each day, or two if the movie is worth your time. You have many options so spread your wings and reach for the sky.

Charlotte Howard is a Woman Entrepreneur, 5x's Best Selling Author, CEO of Charlotte Howard Consulting, LLC, CEO & Founder of Hair Artist Association,LLC, CEO of Heart Centered Women Publishing, Publisher of Hair Artist Lifestyle Magazine and Founding Premier Member of Women Speakers Association. Charlotte is an Internationally renown Radio Host for Success & Beauty Talk Radio Show.

Charlotte is also a certified Award-winning Hair Artist with over a decade of experience specializing in Women Transformational Life Coaching, Beauty Care Strategies, Hair Artistry, Beauty Salon Business Start-up, Marketing and Client Attraction. She is on a mission to empower millions of women to discover fulfillment and happiness in their lives. She is all about women empowering women to create a renewed sense of energy and motivation for enhancing themselves, lives and business from the inside out! For more information visit www.thehairartistassociation.org

Visit www.HairStylistRiches.com to access your FREE Hair Stylist Riches Audio CD!!

www.ingramcontent.com/pod-product-compliance
Lightning Source LLC
Chambersburg PA
CBHW041552220426
43666CB00002B/48